AS A CAT THINKETH

WORDS AND PICTURES

BY JIM PROIMOS

TO _____

FROM _____

DATE _____

For 108 straight days Cleopatra brought her owner a dead sparrow, a record like DiMaggio's 56 game hitting streak, that most experts feel will never be broken.

Fabio, the world's only uncute kitten.

Max, the feline ol' faithful has become the second biggest tourist attraction in Utica, NY, spouting up to 17 hairballs every 33 minutes.

A cat in Oklahoma has been sleeping in the same spot for 12 years without moving, forcing her owners to watch TV on the floor.

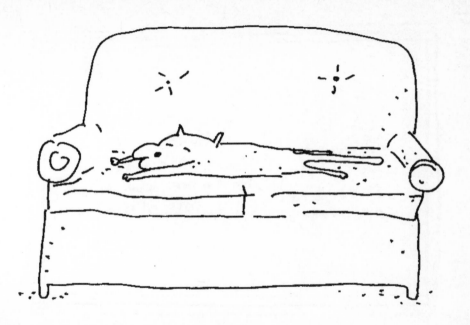

Citizen "Fat Cat" Kane is the weightiest cat on the planet. He's a finicky eater and his owner claims he has a gland problem.

At 127 years old, Rose is the oldest cat in the world. To this day she still smokes and drinks heavily.

Rice Pilaf has appeared in over one thousand commercials and one day hopes to be the first late night talk show host to work from on top of the desk.

Irma Harms of Denver, Colorado has 4,237 cats, all named George.

The smallest cat in existence is Bubba of Reading, PA. 35 Bubbas can fit in the average ball of yarn.

Arnold holds the title "Mr. Scaredy-Cat, USA". Even the sight of Mother Teresa causes him to go into conniptions.

Percicles and his owner set out
to prove that a cat always lands
on its feet, by dropping said
cat from the top of the Berea,
Ohio water tower. Big mistake.

Through the use of his patented
invention, Scientist Ziggy Watson,
has proven that cats do think.
What do they think most?
"Hey, what's this thing attached
 to my head!"

Rolf thinks he's a dog.
Here he is enjoying one of
his favorite activities.

Betsy, from Athens Georgia
has rubbed up against
533,207 legs, slut!

Jethro, a Morris the Cat impersonator, with his owner, Bud Nye, an Elvis impersonator.

A dairy farmer in New Jersey
claims his cat is half feline,
half cow. The only drawback
is that he has to milk her
three times a day.

moo

Katherine has lived over
2,999 lives, all of them
uneventful.

The tallest cat in America is
Whiskers of Forest Hills, NY.
At present he shows no interest
in playing professional basketball.

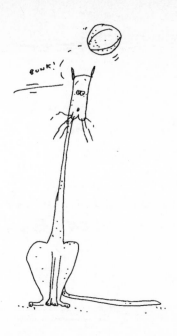

36

In 1987 a woman in West Virginia married her cat. At last check they were still happily married. What's their secret? They lived together first.

Bosco, the cat who inherited one
million dollars several years back
now panhandles in the back alley
behind a mall complex in a suburb
of Seattle. He apparently blew all
his money on fast cars, faster women
and an inordinate amount of squeaky
mouse toys.

17% of cat owners think their pets are actually intelligent life from outer space.

96% of cats think they own their human companions.

Samson has had his tail stepped
on over 5,000 times. Ironically
4,932 have been inflicted by
Jimmy Sands, the boy who
picked him out at the shelter,
thereby saving him from death.

At a fancy restaurant in Fresno, CA
there's a cat who will valet park
your car, and if you ask, recommend
the days best fish entree.

48

You've often heard the famous sound effect of a crash followed by a cat's yelp. That yelp was most likely supplied by unsung recording star, Chrysanthemum.

Garfield's illegitimate son, Tommy.

Pepitone has run onto the field at Yankee Stadium 267 times. And in 1991 was actually credited with a stolen base.

A cat in New Orleans has eaten out of nearly 100,000 trash cans yet still maintains a healthy cholesterol level.

Cats who love dogs who hate cats but live under the same roof, on the next Donahue.

58

Wilma. Cheerful, bright, athletic, likes to snuggle - just don't cross her path!

2,341 bricks have been hurled at Bongo, who nightly sits on a picket fence and sings. To make things worse, what he sings is a medley of Barry Manilow hits.

Friday here is allergic to humans, so turn the page as fast as possible.

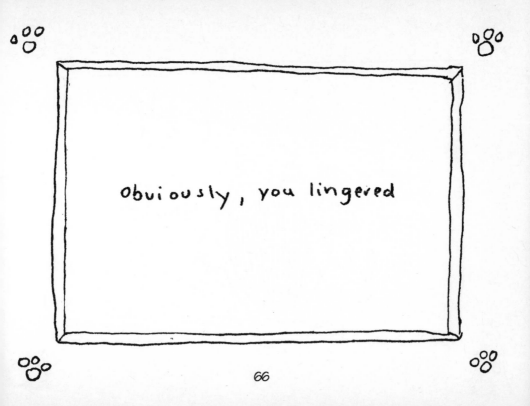

obviously, you lingered

A cat in Chicago, IL has voted in every election since '68. Often more than once.

68

A man in Orlando, FL has named his seven cats after the identically numbered dwarves.

Doc Happy Sleepy

Bashful Dopey Grumpy Sreezy

Selma has been sitting around a
Post Office in downtown Scottsdale,
Arizona for 14 years. Which under
the bylaws of the Postal Worker's
Union entitles her to a hefty check.

If you see this cat please report it to your local authorities. He goes by the name "Babe" and although he seems sweet at first, he is responsible for the disappearance of thousands of left socks.

The fastest cat in North America is shemp. SHe can run twice as fast as the fastest human. Of course, she has to be in the mood.

Marie of Queens, NY was thought to have the worlds longest nails, but it was later revealed they were press-ons.

78

The biggest ears of any cat belong to Boots. She can hear her owner from over 17 miles away. But rarely does she pay it any mind.

80

The cat with the longest whiskers makes Chester, Vermont her home. The whiskers serve no practical purpose and in fact make it almost impossible to drink a bowl of milk with any dignity.

Wellington Rodgers III, a cat who only got into this book because he knows the right people.

Chang and Eng, had, as you might have guessed, identical twin siamese cats.

Jennifer Arno, age six, reported that her cat could actually speak. Upon closer examination it was found that her cat was in reality a stuffed teddy bear and she was ordered to see the school nurse.

88

88

Hitler never had a cat.
Draw your own conclusions.

90

Lumpy King, big time
cat-fight promoter

91

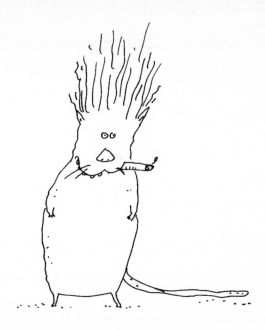

Arnie, the thinest cat in the South west, hails from Carson City , Nevada .

A cat in Flint, Michigan drank 201 gallons of milk in one sitting. But the more amazing thing was she drank that milk straight from the cow.

Over seven million tied for the award given to the world's laziest cat.

Michelle is Nashville's fluffiest feline.
She's so soft that if she were
toilet paper she'd be considered
2 million ply.

The only known poisonous variety of cat is Binky, who occasionally sticks unsuspecting passersby with a very sharp #2 pencil.

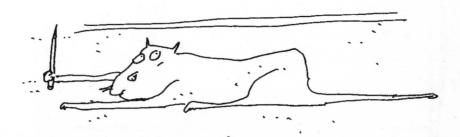

Arnold Catenegger

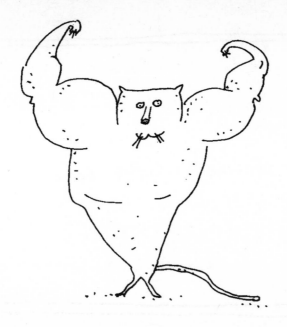

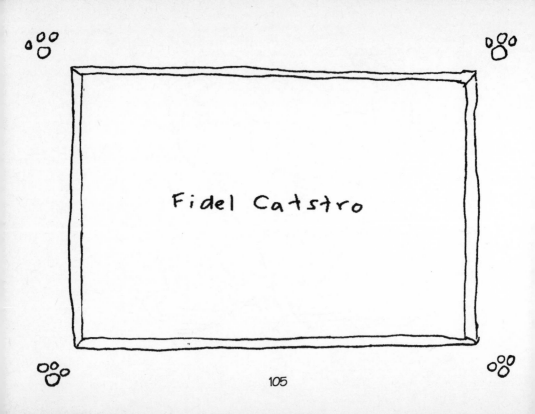

Fidel Catstro

Mother Catresa

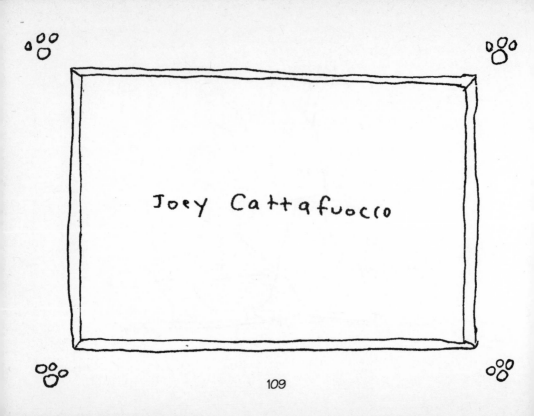

Joey Cattafuocco

H. CAT Perot

Napolean Cataparte

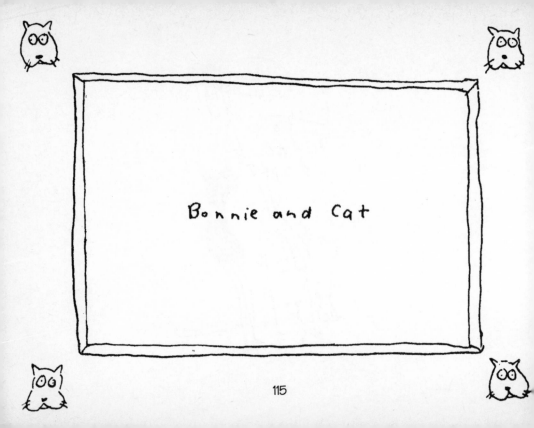

Bonnie and Cat

Mohancat Gandhi

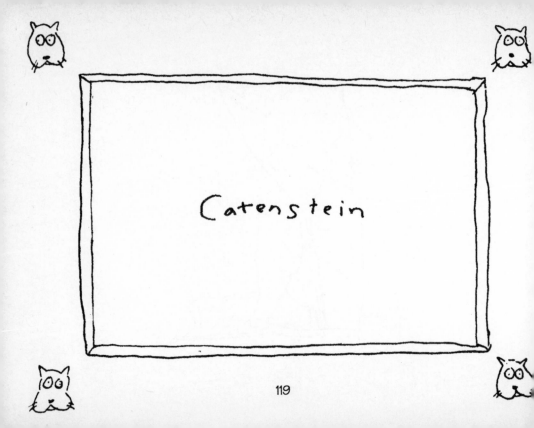

Catenstein

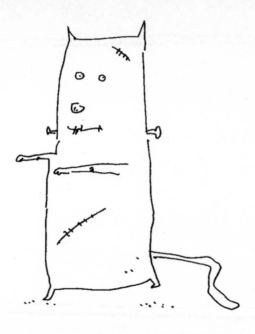

120

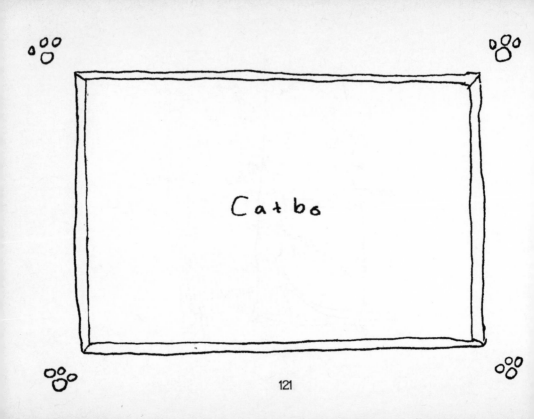

Cat bo

Bud Abbott + Lou Catstello

Andrew "Dice" Cat

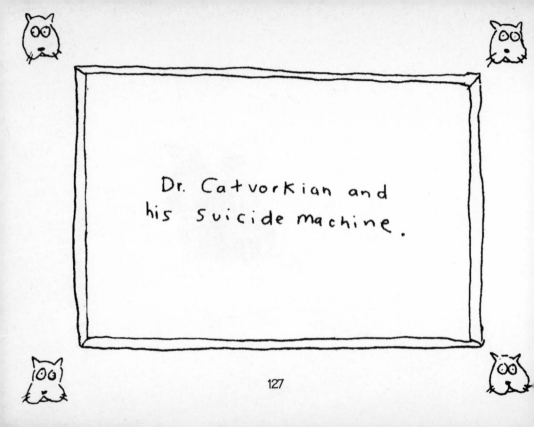

Dr. Catvorkian and his suicide machine.

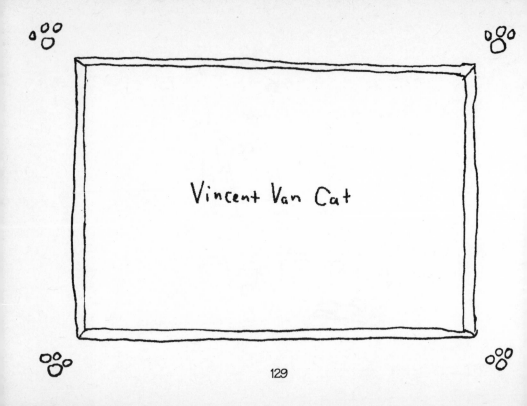

Vincent Van Cat

130

Tammy Faye Cat

Super Model,
Cindy Catford

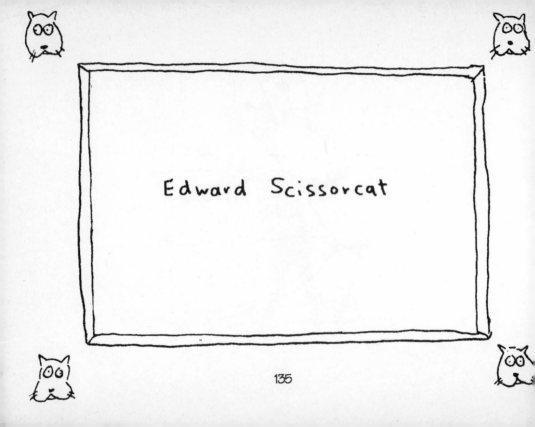

Edward Scissorcat

Mikhail Baryshnicat

138

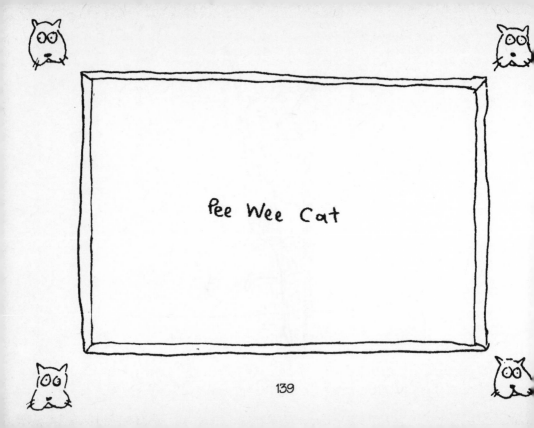

Pee Wee Cat

140

Ted Catson, former "Cheers"
star in career killing black face.

142

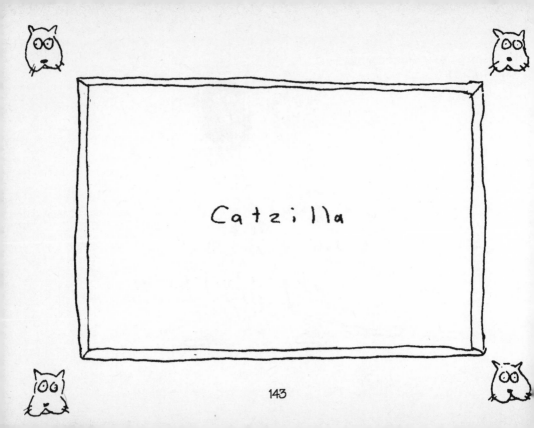

Catzilla

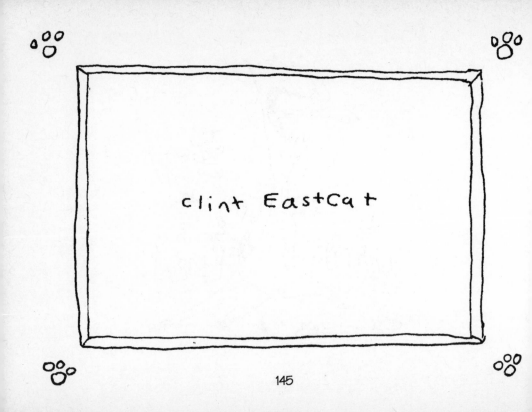

clint EastCat

146

Mr. Spock, from
the Catship Enterprise.

147

148

Stand up
Catmedian.

150

Conehead Cat

152

Big pumkinhead,
Cat Limbaugh.

154

child star,
Macaulay Catkin

Barney, the big lovable, stupid, purple cat that your kids just can't get enough of.